ALEX NOGUÉS is a writer and geologist specializing in groundwater and paleontology. He has written or illustrated over sixty books, including *Stories in a Seashell* (StarBerry Books). He lives in Spain with his family.

MIREN ASIAIN LORA is the illustrator of *Hello, Earth!* and *A Good Day* (both Eerdmans). She studied fine arts at the University of the Basque Country, and her artwork has been shown in several exhibitions in Spain, Argentina, Italy, and Mexico. Miren lives in Spain. Visit her website at miaslo.com.

LAWRENCE SCHIMEL is an author, anthologist, publisher, and translator of books in both Spanish and English. His works have received many awards, including the SCBWI Crystal Kite Award, a PEN Translates Award, and the GLIL Best Translated YA Book Honor. Lawrence lives in Madrid and New York City. Follow him on Twitter @lawrenceschimel.

Eager I hasten to the vale,
As if I heard brave news,
How nature held high festival,
Which it were hard to lose.

Henry David Thoreau

To the Font de l'Obi, to all those who spent
their childhoods there, and to Jaume Gallemí.

A. N.

Eerdmans Books for Young Readers would like to thank Jill Holz (B.S. Geology and Geophysics, M.Ed., and National Geographic Certified Educator) for sharing her expertise on the science of how Earth works.

Text © 2019 Alex Nogués • Illustrations © 2019 Miren Asiain Lora • First published in Spain by Editorial Flamboyant S. L. under the title *Un millón de ostras en lo alto de la montaña* • www.editorialflamboyant.com

Translated from the Spanish by Lawrence Schimel

First published in the United States in 2021 by Eerdmans Books for Young Readers, an imprint of Wm. B. Eerdmans Publishing Co. • Grand Rapids, Michigan www.eerdmans.com/youngreaders • All rights reserved • Manufactured in China

29 28 27 26 25 24 23 22 21   1 2 3 4 5 6 7 8 9

A catalog record of this book is available from the Library of Congress.

AC/E
ACCIÓN CULTURAL
ESPAÑOLA
Support for the translation of this book was provided by Acción Cultural Española, AC/E. www.accioncultural.es.

Illustrations created with gouache on paper

one million oysters

on top of the mountain

ALEX NOGUÉS • MIREN ASIAIN LORA

Translated by
LAWRENCE SCHIMEL

EERDMANS BOOKS FOR YOUNG READERS

Grand Rapids, Michigan

**Let's take a walk. Come with me.
Look around you. What do you see?**

Sure, of course. Who wouldn't spot
the bear and the deer? I suppose
you've also seen the woodpecker, the
salamander, and the *Homo sapiens* with
a hat? But they don't have much to do
with what we're going to talk about.
Let's go on a little further.

And now? Do you see it?

Ha! That's true! That cloud is shaped
like a whale. But no, that's not it.
We can't let the clouds cloud our vision!

And now? Can you see where this is going?

Well, yes. There's a forest. It's lovely.
It's fall. Crops are almost ready to be
harvested. And there's a tractor in the
field. Yes. The stream is marvelous.
Come on, though, let's keep going,
keep going. We've only got a few pages
to explain something amazing.

At last! Can you see the rocks now?

They've been there all along. If you go back, you'll see that they are all around you. And they were there long before the tractor and the man with the hat. Before even the forest and the animals. The landscape is built upon the rocks and is nourished by the minerals in them. The kind of forest that will grow depends in part on the rocks, and what animals will live there depends in part on the kind of forest that grows there.

If the mountains are very tall, they'll push the clouds higher and make them rain. Dawn will come later and twilight will come earlier down in the valley, by the town and the stream.

But why would anyone care about rocks— except for kicking them or skipping them across a lake?

Turn the page: we'll get a little closer.

We're on the top of the mountain. Do you see the outcrop, that bare spot with the rock you didn't notice before? Look at that: it's full of oysters!

....

Oysters?

....

Let's make a list of animals who live in the earth:

Earthworms. Moles. Mole crickets.

In dens we can find mice, badgers, porcupines, and maybe even bears.

....

But oysters?
Oysters live in the sea!
And here in the outcrop
are hundreds, thousands,
millions of oysters!

*How did the oysters get up to
the top of the mountain?*

Did they climb up here?

*Did they fall like rain,
carried by a hurricane?*

*Are they just a bunch of stones that,
by chance, are shaped like oysters?*

....

**I'm afraid not.
The answer is even
more fantastic.**

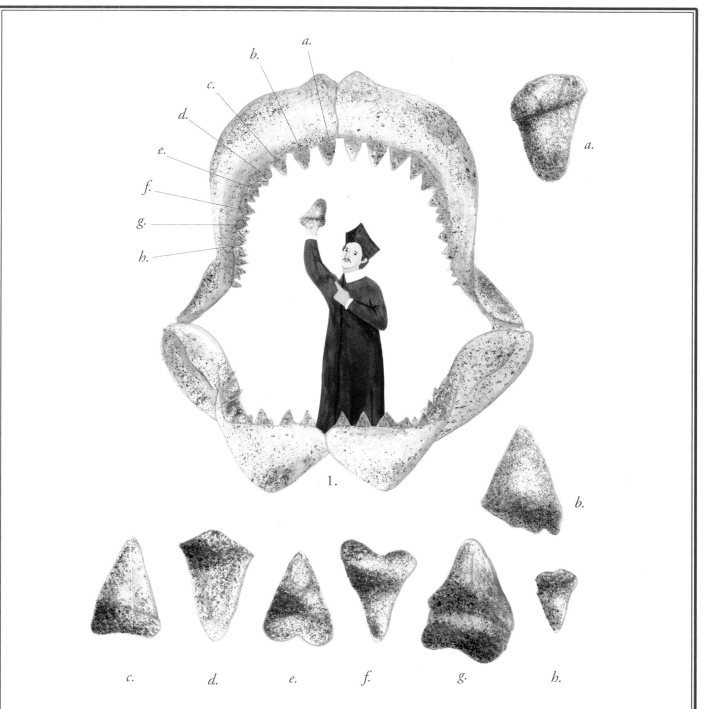

1.

a.

b.

c.   d.   e.   f.   g.   h.

More than 350 years ago, a Danish doctor named Nicolaus Steno noticed something important while dissecting the head of a gigantic 2,600 pound shark. Its teeth caught his attention because they looked remarkably like what were then known as "tongue stones" (glossopetrae).

The glossopetrae were found among rocks. People thought they fell from the sky, and used them as charms against poisons and ailments of all kinds, from fevers to bad breath. But Steno realized that they were actually sharks' teeth. He pondered this a lot—so much, in fact, that because of the ideas and theories that followed this discovery, Steno is considered one of the first geologists in history.

The oysters are fossils. They are the remains
of animals that lived a long time ago,
like this dinosaur.

Shortly after they died, these animals wound up
buried in sediment. They fossilized (turned to
stone) over the course of many, many years,
and thanks to that, they were preserved.

And one day you climb to the top of the mountain and ta-da! You stumble across the oysters.

....

Can you eat them?

....

No. There's nothing left to eat.

....

But how old are they? Is there really no way to count how many years have passed since their death?

....

Maybe.
Let's return to the outcrop.

**Look carefully.
Do you see those lines?
You can follow them
across the landscape.**

The bands of rock between two of these lines are called strata. If the outcrop were a musical score, the strata would be the notes, and the lines would be the pauses in between the notes. The music would begin with lowest part, and end with the highest part.

One of the difficulties in playing this song
is that the thickness of the strata is not
consistent like a musical measure.

Strata don't always last the same amount
of time. And we have the same problem with the
pauses. But the strata, like a music score,
can be read—they have an order, and they can
sing us a song.

Well, that's nice, you must be thinking . . .
*How pretty, really . . . But we want to know
how old the rocks are, not start dancing to
their tune.*

If we brought together all the outcrops on Earth and put that great song of life in order (with the newest strata on top, the oldest down below) we would see that the fossils we find in each layer are different.

In the upper strata, we would find some nearly hairless monkeys that are ancestors to what we currently call humans.

In this layer and the ones below, we might also find other creatures like mammoths and hairy rhinoceroses that have gone extinct—that is, they have died and disappeared from Earth.

Lower down, there are whole lot more extinct mammal fossils.

In the middle, dinosaur and ammonite fossils exist in the rocks.

And in the oldest, deepest layers, there are things as strange as trilobite fossils.

The fossils help us to know what moment of the song we're in. We'll never find a human with a dinosaur in the same stratum, or a trilobite with mammoths. The layers of fossils construct a kind of clock.

Huh. So we know that our oysters are younger than trilobites, but older than mammoths. That doesn't narrow things down much.

Time is measured in seconds, in years, in centuries. It has numbers. No one says, "Let's meet before the last leaf of the oak tree falls, but after the thyme has flowered."

More than a hundred years ago (although that seems like a lot, it's very little, as you'll see by the end of this page) we discovered that certain metals decay at a slow and precise rhythm, emitting radiation that we can capture and measure.

By measuring the radiation of this metal within a stratum, we can know its age quite precisely. Geologists need both the fossil clock and the radiometric clock to know the age of fossils an outcrop.

Now, at last, we can say that our oysters are from the Upper Cretaceous period, and that they lived some 85 million years ago.

Geological time is full of marvelous names that recall places where the strata of those periods or their characteristics were defined.

2.

1.

1. **Devonian** *(from 419 to 359 million years ago):* Devon is a county in the southeast of England where the geologists Murchison and Sedgwick identified this period.

2. **Carboniferous** *(from 359 to 299 million years ago):* During this period, large quantities of carbon were generated in every corner of the world because of the emergence of the first forests (which were very different from current ones).

3. **Permian** *(from 299 to 252 million years ago):* Owes its name to the Russian region of Perm, where Murchison (once again!) defined this period.

4. **Jurassic** *(from 201 to 145 million years ago):* Alludes to the Jura mountains range, near the Alps, the place where the naturalist Alexander von Humboldt identified this period, at the end of the 18th century.

5. **Cretaceous** *(from 145 to 66 million years ago):* Refers to the Latin name for chalk, creta, *which is abundant in the Paris Basin, where this period was defined.*

3.

4.

5.

85 Million Years!

That is a lot of time.

Almost infinitely more than the age of this old woman in China (120 years old). Much, much more than the ruins of the Colosseum in Rome (over 1,900 years old). Even more than the oldest sequoia tree in California (over 3,200 years old).

Careful! The first dinosaurs appeared 230 million years ago; the first trilobites, 520 million years ago; and the first algae began to populate the seas some 1,600 million years ago. Let me write that out with all its zeroes so you can see it better: 1,600,000,000 years ago.

The entire history of human civilization stretches back to just a little over 6,000 years. What could have happened in thousands or millions of years more than that?

Is it possible that oysters from 85 million years ago lived on land?

That would explain everything. Mountain oysters!

But I'm afraid they didn't. The oysters of today are so much like those from 85 million years ago that they must have lived very similar lives. Besides, there's the question of color. Have you noticed?

If a sedimentary rock is black or very dark, it may contain a lot of organic material (such as carbon, petroleum, or compost).

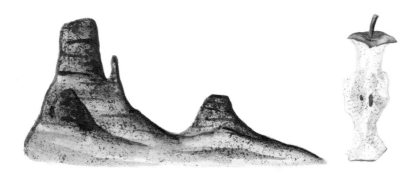

Rocks that are reddish, ochre, or brown have formed as certain minerals have oxidized, or been exposed to the air. The presence of oxygen in nature very often generates reddish colors, like what happens with blood, rust, or the core of an apple that we ate a while ago.

On the other hand, if the sediments are deposited in underwater areas that are somewhat deep, they will take on grayish colors.

There is no doubt: our Cretaceous oysters were aquatic.

**But let's put it to the test.
We'll act like real geologists!**

Let's take a rock.

We'll hit it with a hammer to split it down the middle, and then we'll have a fresh surface.

Splash some water on the surface of the rock. We'll also take an oyster and a handful of the sediment in which it's found, and examine these with a magnifying glass.

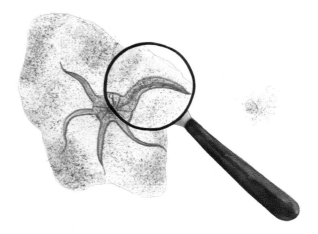

There is an entire world of tiny fossilized marine creatures! The sea, the sea, and more sea. An ancient, warm, tropical sea.

* Water dampens the surface of the rock, and gives contrast so that we can see the rock's details with greater clarity. This is a geological trick that only true geologists use.

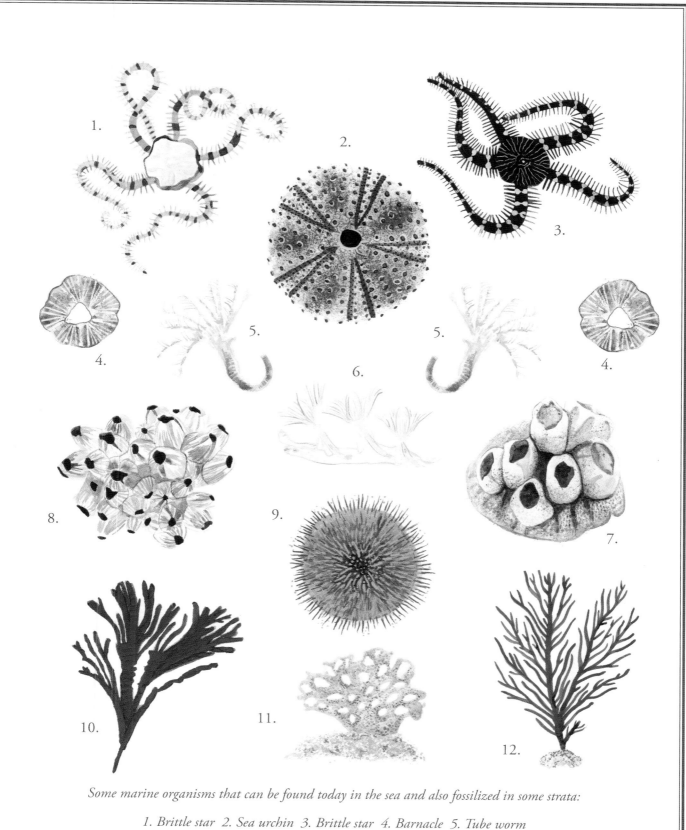

Some marine organisms that can be found today in the sea and also fossilized in some strata:

1. Brittle star 2. Sea urchin 3. Brittle star 4. Barnacle 5. Tube worm
6. Bryozoa 7-8. Barnacle 9. Sea urchin 10. Red algae 11-12. Coral

So now we know that 85 million years ago,
the top of our mountain was a tropical sea.
The oysters didn't climb the mountain,
nor did they fall with the rain,
nor did they just suddenly appear.

The mountain rock was once on the bottom of the ocean floor!

I don't know.
I think that's even harder to understand.
How could the ocean change like that?
A gigantic tsunami?
A universal flood?

Well, neither one of those.

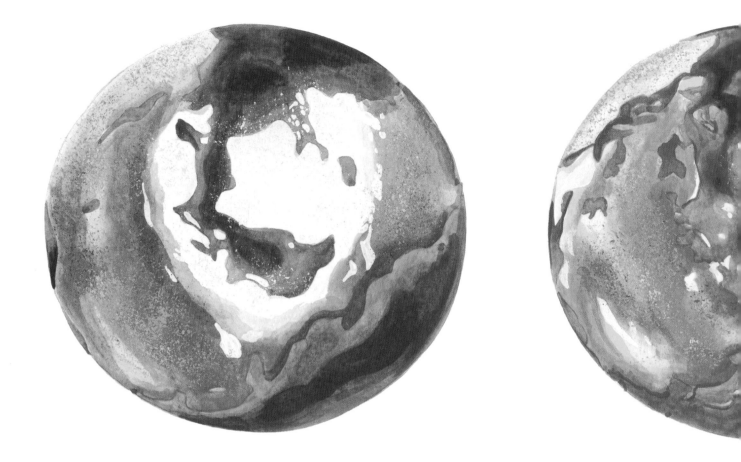

The oceans move. And I'm not referring to the waves and tides.
Oceans move much more than that—they just do so very, very slowly.

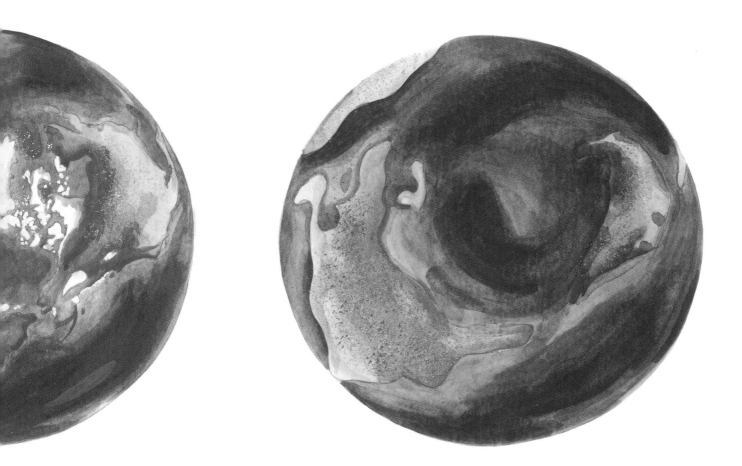

You have probably heard about climate change and the melting of the Arctic. What would happen if all the ice in the world melted? The depth of the oceans would change, and the seas would invade a big part of Earth's coasts. In the past 85 million years, the seas have advanced and retreated many times, leaving behind sediments in the form of strata. That is one of the reasons why the strata are piled one on top of the other, and why they change from red to gray and from gray to red.

An extreme case happened 5.5 million years ago, when the Mediterranean Sea dried up. All of it!

But that doesn't seem to explain how we can find the sea at a height of almost 10,000 feet. There must be something more.

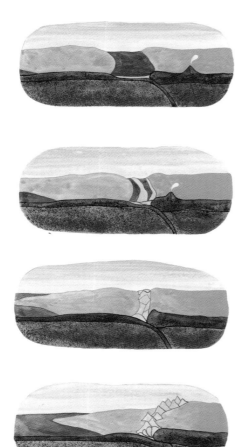

The sea also moves in another, much wilder way.

We live upon a big puzzle of enormous blocks of rock (sometimes as large as continents) which ride on top of the mantle, the layer beneath. When two of these blocks, or plates, wind up pressing against one another as they move, they crash together in super-mega-hyper-slow motion (luckily for us). The rocks wrinkle, they fold, they break. And one plate eventually gives way and sinks toward the mantle, pushed by the other plate, which rides upon its back.

The sediment from the ancient seas is converted into layers of rock. And then it's pushed by violent collisions that happen at such a slow speed that not even the old sequoia noticed. These rocks are moved miles and miles—and the fossils once on the sea floor rise up, up, up . . .

. . . until it turns into the top of a mountain.

Look at all the things these oysters explained to us, despite how ordinary they seemed at first. And that is just the beginning. If you start to listen to the song a little earlier, you'll find a fantastic coral reef. And a few strata lower, the prints of a family of dinosaurs. In other outcrops, perhaps you'll discover animals that you never imagined or that no one has ever seen—or the unmeasurable depths of oceans that no longer exist.

Perhaps you'll step onto the sides of an extinct volcano, or you'll walk into a forest of giant ferns. Wherever you go, you'll find a history, a song, a thousand unexplored worlds waiting for you.

So grab a magnifying glass, a pencil, a notebook, and a hammer, and go for a walk.

GLOSSARY

EARTH'S LAYERS – Earth's outer layer is called the *continental crust*. It is made up of enormous, rigid fragments called *tectonic plates*. These plates move and slide very slowly against each other on top of the *mantle*, a thick layer that is mostly solid—but also hot enough that it can move very slowly like a thick fluid—a sort of bendable solid like Silly Putty. The center of our planet is called the *core*. If you dug a hole to try and reach it, the temperature would increase by between 72° and 87°F every mile, and you'd have to dig some 1,800 miles to reach the surface of the core.

FOSSIL – Means "that which is excavated or dug up." We use the word *fossil* to mean the organic material transformed into stone and found in sedimentary deposits on the Earth's crust.

The remains of organisms (especially those with a mineral composition such as skeletons, shells, and exoskeletons) begin to transform once they are buried. This is due to the effects of water and the changes in pressure and temperature that happens as these organisms are progressively covered beneath more and more sediment. Over the course of thousands and millions of years, the chemical structure of this material changes, turning them into stone.

GEOLOGY – The science that studies the origin, formation, and evolution of the Earth. The word comes from the Greek: *Gaea* (Mother Earth, the daughter of Chaos, in Greek mythology) and *logia*, which means science. *Logia* in turn comes from *logos* (word), so for a more poetic definition we might say that geologists are those who understand the words of Mother Earth or who speak the language of rocks.

OUTCROP – Geologists call places where rock can be seen directly (without vegetation or other obstacles) *outcrops* or *outcroppings*. *Crop* is an old word meaning to rise up from the ground. That is why foods that are cultivated are also called crops, because the plants rise up from the ground.

PALEOMAGNETISM – As we've seen, fossils can serve as a relative clock. Paleomagnestism is another method of telling the age of strata.

Earth is an enormous magnet. The North and South magnetic poles change often (on the scale of millions of years). There are minerals, such as iron, which line themselves up according to Earth's polarity. Scientists can look at the way these minerals have crystalized in rocks and use that as a record of what Earth's magnetic fields looked like when those rocks formed. This can help scientists determine the age of those rocks and learn more about their history.

SEDIMENTARY ROCK – Rocks which are formed by the buildup of fragments of other rocks (sediments) and/or fragments of organic matter on the continental crust. The sand on a beach, for example, is made up of a multitude of tiny fragments of rocks and/or minerals as well as bits of the hard parts of all kinds of animals who live on the coast. If these sediments are buried by new sediments, they can turn into a sedimentary rock over time.

STRATUM (Plural **STRATA) –** This is a strange word that Nicolaus Steno started using to describe what he observed. The word comes from Latin and came to be understood as "that which extends horizontally upon another surface"—for example, a rug. Steno applied three basic laws to the concept, which greatly helped the understanding of rock outcrops and the history of the Earth:

I. The Law of Horizontality – Strata are deposited horizontally, although we might later find the shape or angle changed.

II. The Law of Superposition – The strata we find below are older than the ones we find above.

III. The Law of Lateral Continuity – Strata have the same age throughout their extension.

ALEX NOGUÉS

When I was twelve years old, a curved stick changed my life. My cousins, siblings, and I started to play golf in a stony area. The ball wound up beside a rock with a kind of clam stuck to it. But the sea was fifty miles away, and we were on the edge of a mountain!

Years later, I became a geologist to find the answers to the questions that were born that day. I wandered through Cretaceous seas and found a tiny fossilized organism that no one had ever seen before. The experts called it *Alexina papyracea*,* without knowing that years later books would also play an important role in my life. This book closes the circle. With it I hope to summarize what I have learned, and to share the wonder that comes from learning the language of rocks.

Alexina in recognition of my discovery, *papyracea* for being as thin as papyrus (paper).

MIREN ASIAIN LORA

⋯⋯⋯⋯⋯⋯⋯⋯⋯⋯⋯⋯⋯⋯⋯⋯⋯⋯⋯⋯⋯⋯⋯⋯⋯⋯⋯⋯⋯

As a girl, in the garden next to my house, I found a worm on a leaf. I put it in a jar, and after many days it turned into a butterfly. Magic. That was magic. Life is magic.

Since then, I enjoy observing everything. Looking, seeing, contemplating—how I enjoy doing all of these things! Walking through the forest, spying some creature hidden among the flowers . . . Something new always happens; it is never exactly the same experience.

What pleasure I feel looking at everything!

And now I know that even the rocks have so much to tell me.

How I love nature!